Cowboys

Exeter Books

NEW YORK

A Bison Book

Cowboys

Peter Newark

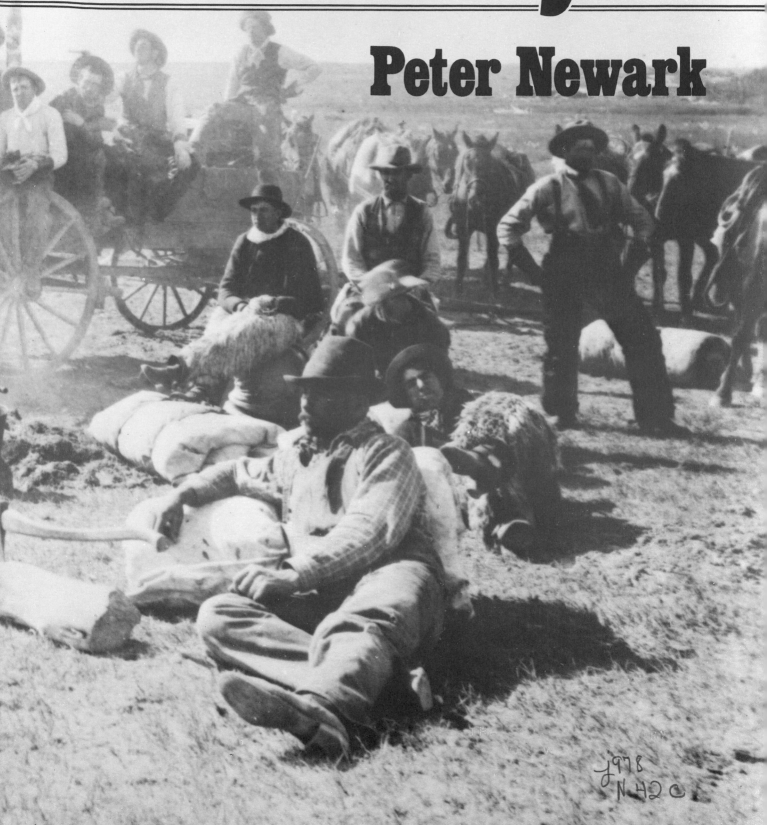

GF

PAGE 1: Morning Sun *by F T Johnson.*
TITLE PAGE: *Wyoming cowboys relaxing near the chuckwagon.*
THIS PAGE: *If there had been such things as typical cowboys, these men might have qualified.* (Men of the Open Range *by C M Russell*)

This book is dedicated to all the unknown working
cowboys who lived and died without fame or favor.

CONTENTS

William F Cody— 'Buffalo Bill'

FOREWORD

The cowboy is the most romanticized, most misrepresented figure ever to ride across the pages of North American history. In the years immediately following the Civil War, the trail-driving cowboy—the original Texas type—quickly gained a reputation for wild behavior and violence, a transient troublemaker, rough and all too ready to use his sixshooter. As the years passed, this desperado was transformed by pulp writers, journalists, and Buffalo Bill's Wild West show into a colorful folk hero. Finally, the alchemists of Hollywood transmuted the base metal of a mounted workingman into an international star of the silver screen, a clean-cut cliché caballero, perhaps best represented by the fanciful figure of Tom Mix.

I do not subscribe to the belief that when truth and legend conflict, print the legend. In writing this factual account of the 19th century cowboy I have drawn largely on newspaper reports and journals of the time, on contemporary views of travelers and observers of the cattle country, and the published recollections of the cowboys themselves. I hereby acknowledge my literary debt to other authors I have consulted and give special thanks to the institutions, museums, friends and strangers who have contributed information and illustrations to this volume. Many of the pictures are from my own extensive collection of Western Americana.

Peter Newark

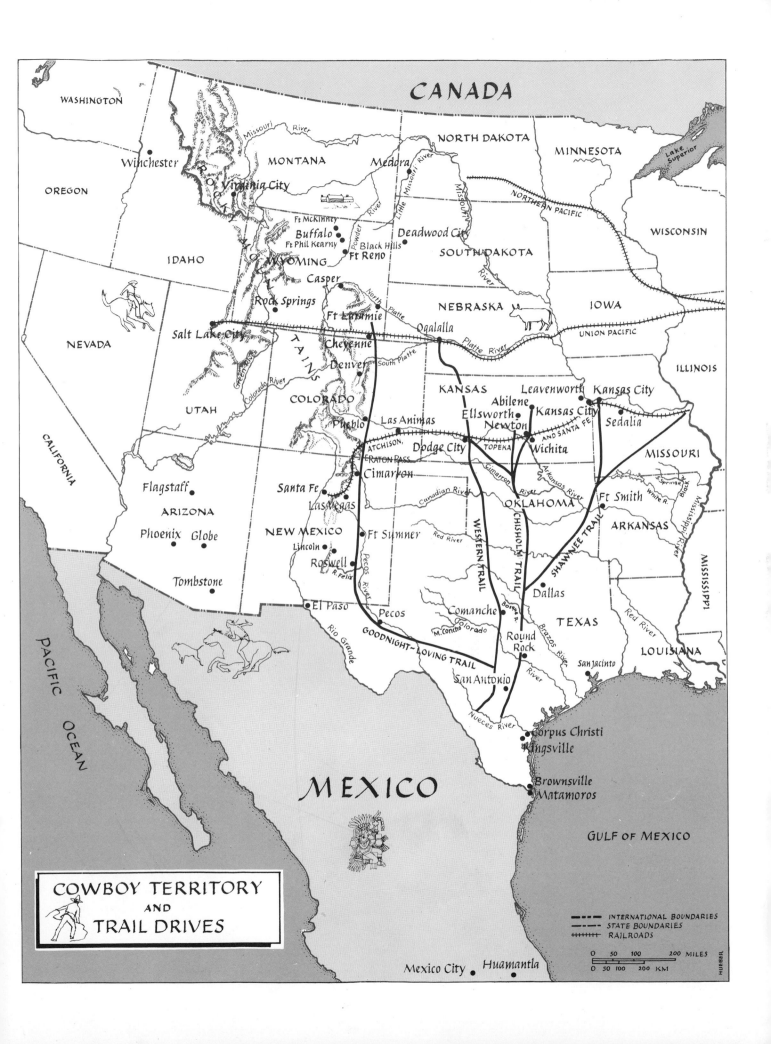

CANADA

WASHINGTON

OREGON

Winchester

MONTANA

NORTH DAKOTA

MINNESOTA

Lake Superior

Medora

Virginia City

Missouri River

Little Missouri River

Missouri River

NORTHERN PACIFIC

WISCONSIN

IDAHO

Ft McKinney

Buffalo

Ft Phil Kearny

Black Hills

Ft Reno

Deadwood City

SOUTH DAKOTA

River

WYOMING

Casper

Rock Springs

Powder River

North Platte

Ft Laramie

Ogalalla

NEBRASKA

IOWA

Salt Lake City

Cheyenne

Platte River

UNION PACIFIC

NEVADA

Denver

South Platte

ILLINOIS

Green River

TAINS

KANSAS

Leavenworth

Kansas City

Colorado River

COLORADO

Las Animas

Abilene

Ellsworth

Newton

Kansas City

Sedalia

UTAH

Pueblo

ATCHISON,

Dodge City

TOPEKA

Wichita

AND SANTA FE

MISSOURI

CALIFORNIA

RATON PASS

Cimarron

Cimarron

Arkansas River

S. Springs

White R.

Black

Flagstaff

Santa Fe

Canadian River

OKLAHOMA

Ft Smith

ARIZONA

Las Vegas

ARKANSAS

MISSISSIPPI

Phoenix

Globe

NEW MEXICO

Ft Sumner

Red River

WESTERN TRAIL

CHISHOLM TRAIL

SHAWNEE TRAIL

Lincoln

Mississippi River

Tombstone

Roswell

R. Felix

Pecos River

Dallas

Comanche

Bosque R.

TEXAS

Red River

El Paso

Pecos

M. Concho

Colorado

Round Rock

Brazos River

LOUISIANA

Rio Grande

GOODNIGHT-LOVING TRAIL

River

San Jacinto

PACIFIC OCEAN

San Antonio

Nueces River

MEXICO

Corpus Christi

Kingsville

Brownsville

Matamoros

GULF OF MEXICO

COWBOY TERRITORY
AND
TRAIL DRIVES

- – – – INTERNATIONAL BOUNDARIES
- – · – STATE BOUNDARIES
- +++++ RAILROADS

Mexico City   Huamantla

0   50   100   200 MILES

0   50 100   200 KM

HUBER

United States Army Dragoons in Texas charging an enemy gun battery in the Battle of Resaca de la Palma, which occurred 9 May 1846 and was a turning point in the Mexican War.

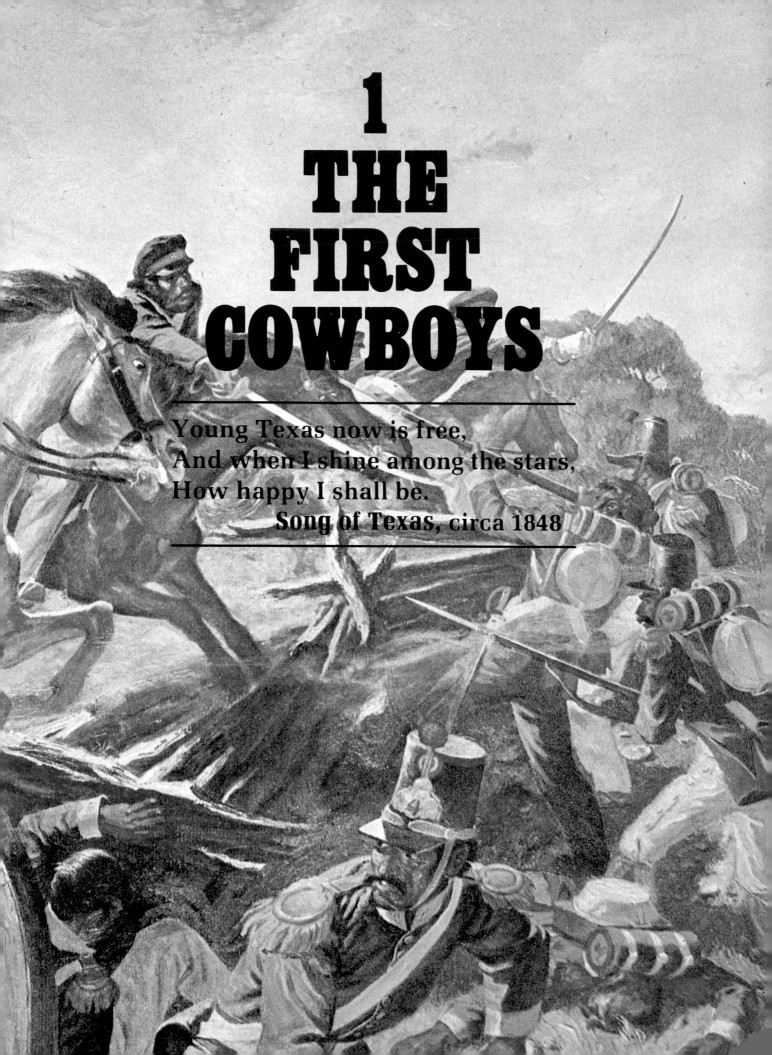

1
THE
FIRST
COWBOYS

Young Texas now is free,
And when I shine among the stars,
How happy I shall be.
Song of Texas, circa 1848

The story of the Anglo-American cowboy begins in Texas, the cradle of the great cattle-raising industry that, in 30 years, fanned out from the Lone Star State to the far northern plains and other Western territories. In the sun-burned wilderness of Texas, frontier man, mustang horse and Longhorn cattle, rawhide and leather, spurs, sombrero and six-shooter coalesced to form the distinctive figure of the Texas cowboy, the paradigm of all other American cowboys that followed him. The Texas cowboy's independent character and Viking spirit were forged in the flames of revolt against Mexican rule and tempered by the Indian-fighting, trouble-shooting tradition of the hard-riding Texas Rangers.

'Cow-boys can be divided into two classes,' commented an observer in 1880. 'Those hailing from the Lone Star State . . . the others recruited either from Eastern States, chiefly Missouri, or from the Pacific slopes . . . The Texans are, as far as true cow-boyship goes, unrivalled; [they are] the best riders, hardy, and born to the business. The others are less able but more orderly men. The bad name of [the] Texans arises mostly from their excitable tempers, and the fact that they are mostly "on the shoot"—that is, very free in the use of their revolvers.'

The original Texas cowboy was a synthesis of Spanish, Mexican and Anglo-American cultures. His particular form owes much to the Spanish occupation of North America and their development of the New World. The Conquistadors and early Spanish colonists introduced domesticated cattle and horses into North America; both types of animal being unknown to the native Indian population. In mastering the mustang, the Plains Indians transformed themselves from a hitherto pedestrian people into skilled equestrian hunters of the bison or buffalo that roamed the prairies in the millions.

The word 'mustang' derives from the Spanish mesteños, meaning horses that had escaped from a mesta or group of stock-raisers. These horses ran wild and multiplied, the Western plains being natural horse (and cattle) country. They evolved into a hardy, wiry, ill-formed breed of small horses, rarely 14 hands (4' 8") high. In similar fashion numbers of Spanish cattle ran off into (or were abandoned in) the wild. They propagated, and evolved into the Texas Longhorn, a distinctive breed of which we shall read more in the following chapter. The Longhorn is the linchpin of the cowboy story; handling these cattle was the way of life of the Texas cowboy.

By the 18th century the aggressive and adventurous Spaniards, greedy for gold and imperial territory, had conquered the whole of Mexico, California and Texas; the latter gaining its name because the Indians were friendly to the Spaniards, who called them tejas, meaning 'friends' or 'allies,' thus the country became known as 'the land of the Tejas,' and later, Texas. Spanish settlers began cattle ranching here, mostly in the triangle of land between the Nueces River, the Rio Grande and the Gulf of Mexico. These ranchos were run in the same free range manner as those in Mexico. The cattle were allowed to wander far and wide over the unfenced open range to graze and breed. And because cattle from different owners intermingled on the plains, a system of branding was introduced to identify the animals by the owner's individual mark. With the grazing animals ranging over such a vast area, horsemen had to be employed to tend and round up the cattle when necessary.

The Spanish ranchers recruited half-civilized mission Indians and halfbreeds to look after the herds. These hardy and humble cow herders were called vaqueros (from the Spanish vaca for cow) and over the years they developed traditional skills and know-how in managing cattle from horseback. They roped the animals with la reata (whence the American 'lariat'), a rawhide rope with a running noose, and they developed gear and equipment suitable to their particular equestrian life. Too poor to afford boots, these early vaqueros strapped huge Spanish spurs to their bare or sandaled feet; and, brought up in the saddle, they seldom walked if they could ride. They wore wide-brimmed hats to ward off the sun and leather aprons to protect their legs from the thorny chaparral brush. Proud of his calling

OPPOSITE TOP: Mexican vaqueros, or cowboys. CENTER: The Spaniards brought cattle into Texas. BOTTOM, LEFT AND RIGHT: Two 19th century illustrations of vaqueros.

and fiercely loyal to his herd and master, the *vaquero* spread his influence throughout the southwest and California.

While the Spanish established their empire on the west coast and in the southwest of North America, the English, Dutch and French colonized the east coast. The English ousted the Dutch and dominated the French. In time the English-speaking colonists rebelled against British rule and created the United States of America. The French still held the vast undeveloped territory of Louisiana, lying between the Mississippi River and the Rocky Mountains, from Canada to the Gulf of Mexico. When in 1803 the United States purchased this great tract of land from France, the size of the infant republic was almost doubled. By the middle of the century streams of wagon trains were rolling westward from the Mississippi carrying settlers to the far wilderness. The Winning of the West had begun.

In 1820 Moses Austin was granted permission by the Spanish authorities to establish a colony of 300 Anglo-American families in the virtually

Cowboys sometimes had problems other than herding cattle, such as occasional attacks by marauding hostile Indians.

uninhabited land of Texas. Moses Austin died before he could carry out his plans and his son Stephen completed the task, settling the families on the rich farm and pasture land along the banks of the Colorado River. When Mexico freed herself of the Spanish yoke in 1821 Texas came under Mexican rule. In those early years Stephen Austin was the undisputed leader of the growing colony, being lawmaker, chief judge and military commander; he dealt with the Indians, charted the province, encouraged industry and promoted commerce with the U.S. and stimulated a steady flow of Anglo-American immigrants into Texas.

The settlers were in constant conflict with the Indians—Lipan, Kiowa, and Comanche—especially the latter. Austin hired a band of horsemen to range over the country to scout the movements of hostile Indians and this duty gave rise to the Texas Ranger force, of which more later. Alarmed at the growing numbers of

Anglos settling in Texas, the Mexican government tried to stop the tide in 1830. This action and other repressive measures (as Anglos viewed it) gave rise to the Texas War of Independence. The new Texans brought with them the industry and thrift that characterized the frontier American, and his spirit of independence and capacity for self-government. The Texans also possessed the Anglo prejudice against the Indian and dislike and contempt for the Spaniard.

From the outset the Texans assumed a racial superiority over the Mexican 'greaser,' a derogatory term that originated in the days when Anglo-American traders bought hides and tallow from the Spaniards in California. In return, the Mexicans referred to the Anglos as 'gringos,' an uncomplimentary name derived from the Spanish *griego* for Greek, meaning a foreigner who spoke 'Greek' or an unintelligible language. Compelling the rebellious Texans to respect Mexican law and government was made extremely difficult because of the colony's isolation from the national capital of Mexico City.

Stephen Austin was imprisoned by the Mexicans for a year and released in 1835. Later that year the Texans rose in revolt and Austin was called upon to command the small volunteer army. He led a successful campaign against San Antonio. In December 1835 he was sent to the US on a diplomatic mission to enlist aid and volunteers. On 23 February 1836 a Mexican army, 5000-strong, commanded by General Antonio Lopez de Santa Ana, President of Mexico, entered San Antonio and laid siege to the fortified mission of the Alamo, held by a garrison of some 180 men, which included the noted frontiersmen James Bowie (of Bowie knife fame) and Davy Crockett. The gallant defenders gave fierce resistance and managed to hold out for 13 days until crushed by the final assault at dawn on 6 March; all the defenders fought to the death. The Mexicans, however, had won a Pyr-

BELOW: A painting by H Charles McBarron entitled The Battle of the Alamo. *INSET: A night view of the floodlit Alamo as it appears today, standing in the heart of downtown San Antonio, Texas.*

14

rhic victory, suffering more than 1500 casualties, causing one of Santa Ana's generals to remark: 'Another such victory and we are ruined.'

Texan vengeance came 46 days after the fall of the Alamo, when General Sam Houston, with an army of less than 800 volunteers, defeated Santa Ana and his army of 1300 at San Jacinto. Before joining battle, Houston exhorted his men: 'Some of us may be killed, must be killed; but, soldiers, remember the Alamo! The Alamo! The Alamo!' The Texans fought with such ferocity that they completely routed the Mexicans in a matter of minutes, killing 600 while losing only eight. This stunning triumph freed Texas from Mexican rule and a Republic was declared in October 1836, with Sam Houston its first president.

The early Anglo settlers in Texas were primarily farmers, and cattle ranching was at first not important to them. With the establishment of the Republic of Texas, the Mexican ranchers, under harrassment from encroaching Texans, abandoned their *ranchos* and many of their cattle and retired to safety over the Rio Grande. The Texans moved into the cattle country and took over the property and stock the Mexicans had left behind. When the new

ABOVE (LEFT TO RIGHT): Stephen Fuller Austin (1793–1836), the colonizer who was called 'The Founder of Texas'; Captain Samuel Walker, who helped design the Walker-Colt revolver; W J 'Bill' McDonald, a famous captain of the Texas Rangers. OPPOSITE: Texas Rangers of the 1890s. LEFT TO RIGHT: Bob Speaker, Jim Putnam, Lon Odam and Sergeant John R Hughes.

republic declared all unbranded cattle public property, Texans, assisted by remaining *vaqueros*, began to round up the wild Longhorns and brand them with their own marks. These Anglo range riders adopted and adapted the methods, dress and equipment of the *vaquero*, and many of the Spanish-Mexican words he used, and in the following years developed the skills, character and life style that comprised the Texas cowboy.

But why the name 'cowboy' in particular? Why not 'cowman' or 'cow herder,' or 'stock boy' or 'cow driver' or 'trail rider'? Well, indeed they were called all these things in their time but 'cowboy' is the one that stuck and came into general use about a century ago. It is an appropriate appellation, as most cowboys were young. The term started to appear in the popular press about 1870 and for a number of years

it was always hyphenated and enclosed in quotation marks. A journalist of 1873 informed his readers that 'The "Cow-Boys" of Texas are a peculiar breed. They are distinct in their habits and characteristics from the remainder of even the Texas population as if they belonged to another race. The Lipan and Comanche are not unlike the civilized white man than is the nomadic herdsman to the Texan who dwells in the city or cultivates the plains.'

The origin of the term 'cowboy' can be traced back to Revolutionary days, when guerrillas plundered the New York area stealing supplies and livestock for the British. In the *Pictorial Field Book of the Revolution* published in 1850, Benson Lossing tells us that 'The party called Cow-Boys were mostly refugees belonging to the British side, and engaged in plundering the people near the lines of their cattle and driving them to New York.' The first use of the term in Texas is open to argument. Some say it was applied to a wild bunch of riders led by Ewen Cameron who harassed the Mexican ranchers and fought the Indians during the early days of the Texas Republic and became known as 'Cameron's Cowboys.'

It seems that early Texas usage of the name 'cowboy' was synonymous with 'bandit' or 'robber.' Charles W Webber in *Tales of the Southern Border*, 1868, writes: 'The old man was a cattle driver, or "cow-boy," as those men are and were termed who drove in the cattle of the Mexican *rancheros* of the Rio Grande border, either by stealth, or after plundering or murdering the herdsman. They were, in short, considered as banditti before the Revolution, and have been properly considered so since.' After the Civil War, 'cowboy' came to signify anyone who tended cattle out West, but the name still retained a connotation of wildness; it was much, much later that 'cowboy' spelled romantic adventure.

The popular term 'cowpuncher' came into use in the mid-1880s when cowboys employed prodpoles to urge cattle through chutes into railroad cars, and often had to 'punch' those animals onto their feet that had got down in the crowded car; 'cowpoke' is another version of cowpuncher. A cowboy was also called a 'buckeroo,' a corruption of *vaquero*. 'Cattleman' and 'rancher' were always used to denote an owner or raiser of cattle; at the top of the league were the 'cattle kings' or 'barons.'

'The original cow-boy of this country,' wrote Joseph Nimmo, Jr, in *The American Cow-Boy*, in the November, 1886 issue of *Harper's New Monthly Magazine*, 'was essentially a creature of circumstance, and mainly a product of western and south-western Texas. Armed to the teeth, booted and spurred, long-haired, and covered with the broad-brimmed sombrero—the distinctive badge of his calling—his personal appearance proclaimed the sort of man he was. The Texas cow-boys were frontiersmen, accustomed from their earliest child-hood to the alarms and the struggles incident to forays of Indians of the most ferocious and warlike nature. The section of the State in which they lived was also for many years exposed to incursions of bandits from Mexico, who came with predatory intent upon the herds and the homes of the people of Texas . . . But the peculiar characteristics of the Texas cow-boys qualified them for an important public service. By virtue of their courage and recklessness of danger, their excellent horsemanship, and skill in the use of firearms . . . they have been efficient in preventing Indian outbreaks and in protecting the frontier settlements.'

The Texas Rangers are part and parcel of the Texas cowboy story. The Rangers were the first to adopt Samuel Colt's early revolver; many cowboys volunteered for Ranger service and many Rangers, after their period of service, took up ranching. John R Hughes was a cowboy, a rancher, then a Ranger. Born in Illinois, he went to the Indian Territory (Oklahoma) and lived with the Indians for several years, learning to track animals and men. In 1878, working as a cowboy in Texas, he drove cattle up the trail to Kansas. He then started his own horse ranch in central Texas. In 1884 thieves ran off 70 of his horses and Hughes went after the gang alone. After a long trail he caught up

LEFT: *An advertisement for Colt firearms painted in 1925 by Frank E Schoonover.* ABOVE: *One of the dangers of the cattle drive was the ever-present possibility of a stampede (*Cattle Stampede *by Robert Lindneux).*

BELOW: *The buffalo was almost extinct by 1900 (*The Still Hunt *by J H Moser, 1888).* RIGHT: *An Eastern view of the rough and ready men of the West—a cartoon of 1861 showing a wild and hairy Texas Ranger loaded with his weapons.*

with the six men in New Mexico and in the ensuing gunfight killed four of them and, in his own words, 'took the two surviving robbers to the nearest town and delivered them to the authorities.' He returned to his ranch with the stolen horses, having been away just under a year and traveling 1200 miles. It was this incident that led him to join the Rangers, in which he served for 28 years, from 1887 to 1915, and rose to the rank of captain. Such was his reputation in the force that journalists dubbed him the 'Bayard of the Chaparral' and 'Boss of the Border.'

W J 'Bill' McDonald, former cowboy and rancher, was a celebrated Ranger captain of the 1890s. He embodied the fighting spirit of the force. It is said that on one occasion when called on to deal with a mob situation he turned up alone. 'Where are the other Rangers?' asked the local authority.

'You ain't got but one riot, have you?' replied the taciturn McDonald.

His tenacious courage was best demonstrated when he engaged in a gunfight with three desperadoes led by a man named Mathews. Having been shot in the lung by Mathews, the Ranger fired back and fatally wounded the man. Then the other two gunmen started shooting at McDonald, hitting him twice in the left arm and in the right side. With the fingers of his gun hand numbed, the Ranger could not cock the hammer of his single-action Colt, so he raised the revolver to his mouth and pulled back the hammer with his teeth; this determined action so unnerved his opponents that they turned and fled. McDonald recovered from his wounds and in 1897 was instrumental in smashing the notorious Bill Ogle gang of San Saba County.

> He ne'er would sleep within a tent,
> No comforts would he know;
> But like a brave old Texican,
> A-ranging he would go.
> *Ballad of Mustang Gray*

The Texas Rangers originated in 1823 when Stephen Austin hired a band of horsemen to range over the country to scout the movements of hostile Indians, and this ranging duty gave the name to the force that became fully established during the period of the Texas Republic,

1836—45. Organized into companies with a captain commanding each company, the Rangers were self-reliant individuals who knew no military discipline; they never drilled or saluted their officers, and accepted a leader only if he proved the best in endurance, courage, and judgment. They wore no uniform and dressed in frontier style. Each man provided his own horse and equipment. What they lacked in military discipline they made up in remarkable riding and fighting ability. A Texas Ranger was defined as one who 'can ride like a Mexican, trail like an Indian, shoot like a Tennessean, and fight like a devil!'

For half a century the Rangers engaged in a continuous war with the fierce Comanches, probably the finest horsemen among the Plains Indians. In the early years the single-shot muzzle-loaded guns of the Rangers were inadequate against the bow and arrows of the Comanche, who could discharge a stream of arrows at his foe while at the gallop. The Rangers gained a great advantage over the Indians when they came into possession of Samuel Colt's revolver, an early five-shot model. Armed with two of these revolvers, one Ranger now had the firepower of 10 men armed with a single-shot weapon. The Colt was an ideal horseman's weapon and the Rangers used it with surprising and devastating effect against the Indians.

The first battle in which Colt revolvers were used against the Comanches took place at Pedernales in June 1844 when Captain Jack Coffee Hays and 14 Rangers clashed with about 70 redskins. The Comanches were accustomed to facing single-shot weapons, and when these had been discharged and were being reloaded, the Indians would charge. But this time, instead of taking up a defensive position, Hays led his men in a spirited charge, taking heavy toll at close quarters with their repeating pistols. More than 30 Indians were killed and the others put to flight. Hays modestly gave the credit for the victory to the 'wonderful marksmanship of every Ranger, and the total surprise of the Indians, caused by the new six-shooters, which they had never seen or heard of before.'

The first six-shot Colt revolver was the .44 caliber 'Walker' Model of 1847, so called because Samuel Colt designed the weapon along lines suggested to him by Ranger Captain Samuel H Walker. The US government ordered 1000 of this new model for use in the Mexican War of 1846-48, a war triggered when Texas joined the Union in 1845 and the United States

BELOW LEFT: In an illustration from the 1880s, two Texas Rangers arrest a Mexican outlaw in a Texas cantina. BELOW RIGHT: R H Williams, an Englishman who moved to Texas to run a ranch and later joined the Texas Rangers.

claimed the Rio Grande as its southern boundary with Mexico. The Mexicans disputed this and war resulted. Since the Rangers had long experience in fighting the Mexicans, General Zachary Taylor employed them as scouts and skirmishers. Captain Sam Walker, according to N C Brooks, in *A Complete History of the Mexican War*, 1849, used his Walker Colt with great effect:

'Foremost of all in this noble charge was the gallant Walker. Firing his revolvers with a cool, steady, equable movement, his unerring hand brought down an enemy with every shot . . . he kept his place in the advance, and whenever the enemy attempted to make a stand, dashed upon him with a cry of triumph, and tore a bloody pathway through.' Walker was killed in action at Huamantla in October 1847: 'He died with a smoking Colt revolver in his hand.'

The United States won the war, which was formally ended by the Treaty of Guadalupe Hidalgo in February 1848. Mexico lost far more than a war. By the terms of the treaty she relinquished all claims to Texas above the Rio Grande, and ceded to the US the lands of New Mexico (including the present states of Arizona, New Mexico, Utah, Nevada, and parts of Wyoming and Colorado) and Upper California (the present State of California). In return for this vast acquisition, the victorious United States agreed to pay Mexico 15 million dollars. The Colt revolver attained national fame in the Mexican War. Indeed, the Rangers' enthusiasm for the weapon had saved Samuel Colt from going out of business for lack of orders.

'I am indebted to Texas,' Colt wrote in a letter to Sam Houston, 'for the development of the advantages my arms possess over the common arms of service. To Texans, I owe the orders I received for arming the first regiment of US Mounted Rifles of which the celebrated Colonel Walker holds a Captain's Commission. I am also indebted to Colonel Hays and other distinguished Texas officers now raising regiments and companies to fight in Mexico for late applications and requisitions on our Government for these arms . . . Texas has done more for me and my arms than all the country. Besides, they have a better knowledge of their use and want

ABOVE: Three Texas cowboys trying to rope a longhorn steer while their partners are tending the rest of the herd. OPPOSITE: Breaking a horse was an important job (The Bronco Buster by Frederic Remington). INSET: Cattle Drive from Texas.

TOP: An illustration by Frederic Remington from an issue of Harper's New Monthly Magazine, 1896, *showing Texas Rangers attacking a Comanche Indian village.* LEFT: *Texas Ranger J B Armstrong, who captured the outlaw John Wesley Hardin in 1877.*

dations of the Comanches. Charles Goodnight, cowboy and later cattle king, served in the Rangers during this period. With the Civil War over, Texans returned to find their state in an economic depression. Farms, ranches, and industries were run down and neglected. Confederate money was now useless. The only assets readily available were the Longhorn cattle which, untended during the war years, had proliferated to the enormous number of some five million head. Texas was poor but had this great reservoir of beef. The north was rich in industry but short of meat to feed its huge and hungry population. So began the period of the long trail drives north from Texas that is dealt with in the following chapter.

The end of the Civil War also brought a time of lawlessness to Texas. The Reconstruction forces took over the Texas government and the State had little control over its own destiny. The Ranger strength was reduced and a new state police force established, a force that proved to be corrupt, inefficient and widely despised. As a result the frontier became unsafe and Mexi-

every Texas Ranger, in Mexico, to be thus armed before they are furnished any other troops.'

Thus did the Colt six-shooter and the Texas Ranger become inseparable. And the Colt and the cowboy became synonymous. When Texas seceded from the Union in 1861 and many Texans marched off to serve the Confederacy, the Rangers had to fight hard to protect the isolated, unmanned communities from the depre-

can bandits were encouraged to cross the Rio Grande and steal cattle. When Texas outlaw John Wesley Hardin was interviewed in jail in 1877 he told the reporter that his first trouble with the law had come with the state police: 'The Yankees and the state police got after me and tried to arrest me without a warrant.' The state police was abolished in April 1873, much to the delight of all Texans. 'The people of Texas,' announced the *Dallas Herald*, going on to mix metaphors in grand style, 'are today delivered from as infernal an engine of oppression as ever crushed any people beneath the heel of God's sunlight.'

In 1874, when the Texas legislature was returned to the hands of responsible men, a bill was passed creating six companies of Rangers to be known as the Frontier Battalion, at the same time another company was formed as the Special Force. The Frontier Battalion was raised to serve against the Indians on the Western frontier; the Special Force, commanded by Captain L H McNelly, was given the duty of ridding south Texas of the many Mexican cattle thieves and other outlaws. McNelly carried out his duty with ruthless efficiency. In June, 1875 he intercepted a band of Mexicans driving a herd of stolen cattle. Here is part of his report on the fight:

'The Mexicans then started at a full run, and I found that our horses could not overtake them. So I ordered three of my best mounted men to pass to their right flank and press them so as to force a stand. And as I had anticipated, the Mexicans turned to drive my men off, but [the Rangers] held their ground, and I arrived with four or five men, when the raiders broke. After that it was a succession of single hand fights for six miles before we got the last one. Not one escaped out of the twelve that were driving the cattle. They were all killed. I have never seen men fight with such desperation . . . I lost one man . . . We captured twelve horses, guns, pistols, saddles, and 265 head of beef cattle belonging in the neighborhood of King's Ranch, Santa Gertrudis.'

John Wesley Hardin, credited with killing 40 men, eluded capture until August, 1877 when he was arrested in Florida by Texas Ranger J B Armstrong. On learning Hardin's whereabouts, Armstrong obtained the necessary warrants and permission from local authorities and boarded the train on which the outlaw was travelling with some companions. Armstrong drew his .45 Colt Peacemaker which had a 7½-inch barrel. On seeing this revolver, in particular use with the Rangers, Hardin cried, 'Texas, by God!' and went for his own pistol—but the gun got snagged in his suspenders! One of Hardin's companions sent a bullet through Armstrong's hat and the Ranger promptly shot the man dead. Determined to take Hardin alive, Armstrong grabbed for the killer's gun, but was kicked backward into an empty seat. Armstrong then knocked Hardin unconscious with his Colt. He disarmed the other men and returned to Texas with Hardin, who received a long prison term.

A year after Hardin's capture, Ranger Colts took the life of notorious outlaw Sam Bass in a shoot-out at Round Rock, Texas. The Special Force was disbanded in 1881 and the Frontier Battalion in 1901, when the service was reorganized as the Texas Ranger Force to meet the changing requirements of the 20th century. While the Rangers were chasing Indians and bandits, the Texas cowboy was stamping his own brand on American history. The trail-driving years brought these 'weather-beaten rough riders' to the notice of the nation at large. 'With the great annual cattle drives which start from the arid plains of the Red River and the Pecos,' ran an article in *Harper's New Monthly Magazine* of July 1884, 'comes the wild cow-boy, with his six-shooter on his hip and his leathern [gunbelt] bristling with little metal cylinders.' It has been estimated that from 1866 to 1895 some ten million Longhorns were driven north from the land of the Lone Star flag, giving a special meaning to the couplet:

> Other states were made or born,
> Texas grew from hide and horn.

The ominous clouds in the background may indicate approaching trouble in the painting, Cattle Drive, by James Walker.

2
THE TRAIL DRIVES

Over the prairies wide and brown,
On through the wilds where there ain't no town.
Swimming the rivers that bar our way,
Trailing the cattle day after day.
Traditional cowboy song

The Texas Longhorn, fierce and feral, was the bedrock on which the great cattle country of the Southwest was founded. The Longhorns of the trail driving years were incredibly hardy creatures, able to thrive on little sustenance. In appearance they were slab-sided, rawboned and rangy with a thick tough hide, mostly black or dark brown in color. Steers carried a pair of horns with an average spread—tip to tip—from three to five feet. Its beef was not as good as that of corn-fed domestic cattle, but Texas had Longhorns in the millions and the meat fed the factory workers in the cities, the construction crews that built the railroads, the gold and silver miners of the West, and the reservation Indians. Longhorns were also driven to the Northern Plains to stock the vast open ranges there, thus spreading the cattle industry far and wide.

The ancestry of this significant beast can be traced through the black fighting bulls of Spain —descendants of the cattle driven into that country by the Moors—to the extinct auroch forebears of all European cattle. The first domestic cattle to arrive in the New World came with Columbus on his second trip to Santo Domingo in 1493; and the little black cattle were among the livestock of Gregorio de Villalobos when he came to Mexico as Viceroy of New Spain in 1521.

Wherever the Spanish ventured in the New World, cattle went with them. On moving into regions north of the Rio Grande in the late 17th and early 18th centuries they stocked their Missions and *ranchos* with Spanish cattle. Indian raids and the open range encouraged many of these animals to escape into the wild. There they rapidly increased in numbers and developed the characteristics that enabled them to survive and flourish on the arid ranges of the Southwest. The Texas Longhorn evolved from these wandering herds, a distinctly North American breed resulting from natural selection and adaption to environment. In the period between the Texas revolution and the Civil War the wild Longhorns became so numerous that they had little value in the Lone Star State.

Trail driving began in the late 1830s when herds of from 300 to 1000 were gathered in the Nueces and Rio Grande country and driven to markets in the cities of the interior. In 1842 a herd of 1500 was trailed to Missouri; that same year the driving of cattle to New Orleans began. In 1846 Edward Piper drove 1000 head to Ohio. In 1850 drives began to California to get beef to the gold miners who were pouring into the Eldorado state. Six years later came the first drive from Texas to Chicago. These trail drives ended with the outbreak of the Civil War and the Longhorns, untended, proliferated greatly on the ranges. It has been estimated that at the close of the Civil War, 1865, there were five million Longhorns in Texas. And these cattle were almost the only source of revenue in the state.

In Texas, Longhorns were sold as cheaply as three or four dollars a head, and even at that rock-bottom price there were few buyers in the state. In the meat hungry north, whose livestock had been greatly depleted by the demands of the Civil War, Texas cattle could fetch 40 dollars a head. Over the next 25 years some 10 million head were driven northward from the 'Longhorn State,' mostly over the Goodnight-Loving Trail, the Chisholm Trail, and the Western Trail. In 1866 approximately 260,000 Longhorns were driven across the Red River for the northern markets, chiefly over the Shawnee Trail to Sedalia, Missouri, the railhead to St Louis and other cities. But this trail, crossing as it did the domesticated cattle land of southeastern Kansas and Missouri, brought troubles and danger to the Texas drovers. The cause of the problems was the parasite tick carried by the Longhorns that spread the deadly Texas or Spanish fever among the resident northern cattle. The Longhorns were immune to the disease.

The menace was acknowledged by Kansas and Missouri farmers before the outbreak of the Civil War and they had actively opposed the entry of Texas cattle. Now, in 1866, they did so again, with even more vigor. This resentment was compounded by the activity of armed gangs of ruffians and robbers who, under the pretext of guarding the land against the dreaded fever, preyed on the Texas cowboys. 'The southwestern Missouri roads leading to Sedalia were the scenes of the worst work of these outlaws,' wrote Joseph McCoy in his book on the cattle trade published in 1874. 'When outright murder was not resorted to as the readiest means of getting possession of a herd, drovers were flogged until they promised to abandon their stock, mount their horses, and get out of the country as quick as they could.' And once having obtained possession of the cattle, McCoy commented, the robbers seemed to lose all fear of the fever and went on to sell them, pocketing the proceeds themselves.

Faced with this flagrant thieving activity, and with the farmers' and grangers' demands for stricter quarantine legislation, the situation was fast becoming impossible for the Texans who wanted the eastern cities' market. Joseph McCoy provided the solution in 1867 when he es-

Occasionally there was time for entertainment on the trail. Cowboys singing around the campfire in 1910.

ABOVE: *After the drive, the cowboys wanted some fun (In Without Knocking by Charles M Russell).* BELOW: *Loading Texas cattle into railroad cars at a Kansas railhead in the 1870s.*

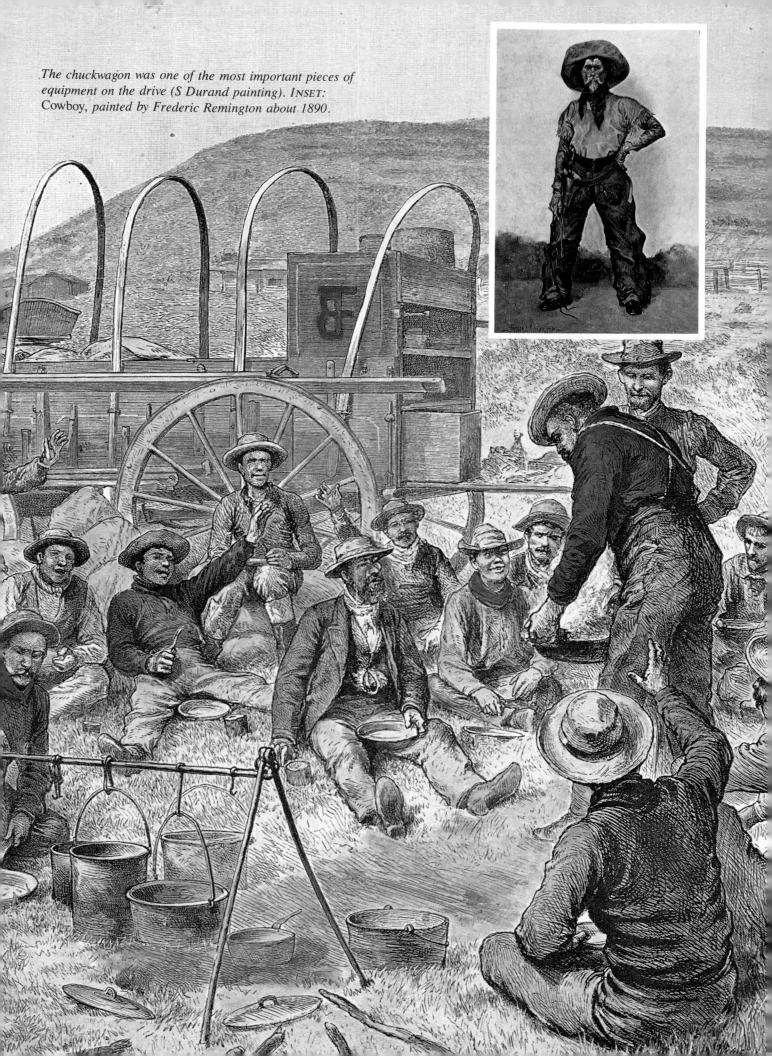

The chuckwagon was one of the most important pieces of equipment on the drive (S Durand painting). INSET: Cowboy, painted by Frederic Remington about 1890.

32

tablished Abilene in Kansas as a trouble-free railhead depot for Texas cattle, and publicized the route pioneered by Jesse Chisholm, a half-breed trader. With its tap roots in Southern Texas, the Chisholm Trail ran north right across central Texas, on through the Indian Territory (Oklahoma) and halfway across Kansas (a region where the quarantine strictures did not apply) to Abilene.

The long trail crossed a number of major rivers, the Colorado, the Brazos, the Red River, the Cimarron, the Canadian and the Arkansas. It was a popular route with the Texans, embracing the best fords and water holes, with plenty of grass for the cattle to feed on. Between 1867 and 1871 some 1½ million Longhorns passed over the Chisholm Trail to Abilene. 'From 200 to 400 yards wide, beaten into the bare earth, it reached over hill and through valley for over 600 miles,' wrote an old time cowboy describing the Chisholm Trail. 'A chocolate band amid the green prairies, uniting the North and the South. As the marching hoofs wore it down and the wind and the waters washed the earth away, it became lower than the surrounding country.'

Initially, Texas cattle were shipped to the meat plants of the east, via the succeeding railheads in Kansas; later herds were sent to stock, or to fatten on, the rich grasslands of the northern plains. The higher prices Chicago meat companies were willing to pay for cattle fattened on northern ranges increased the northward flow in the 1870s. When Dodge City became the major railhead in Kansas it was serviced by the Western Trail, which also extended to the cattle town of Ogalalla, Nebraska, and into Dakota Territory. It took three months to trek a herd from San Antonio to Abilene, six months from Texas to the northern plains. The Goodnight-Loving Trail struck west through Texas, then swung north through New Mexico, Colorado, and into Wyoming. The trail drive, arduous and unromantic though it was in reality, appealed to many young Texans who yearned for adventure, to see places other than their home range. Jim Herron, in *Going Up the Texal Trail*, describes his joining a trail crew in 1880 when he was but 14 years old:

'I had always wanted to be a real cowboy. The Western Trail passed close to the range where we held Father's cattle. Many big herds passed that way daily in the summer months. One day a herd came swinging into sight. I learned that this herd was heading for the Black Hills of Dakota . . . When I rode up [to the trail boss] I asked, "You need a good man?" The boss stood high in his stirrups and shaded his eyes with one hand, all the while looking across the prairie. "Wheah is this man?" he asked. "I sho' don't see him." The two men with him howled with laughter.' Despite the joshing, Herron was hired and when a veteran cowboy warned him that he ran the risk of getting scalped by Indians, Herron boldly replied, 'I'm bound to be a cowboy, even if I have to be a bald-headed one.'

Open range cattle wandered freely over a wide area in search of forage. Few ranchers had full legal title to the land they called their own; each cattleman claimed a certain region of the plains as his range according to the number of cattle he owned and his priority of use. The ranges were unfenced and cattle from different outfits intermingled, therefore the animals were branded to determine ownership. The spring roundup was the gathering together and sorting of the scattered cattle in preparation for the trail drive north. The cowboys and vaqueros would sweep the wide country, searching for and surrounding the dispersed Longhorns and driving them to a point of concentration. In Texas the roundup was especially difficult, with the cattle concealed in thick brush and cactus country, mesquite and chaparral jungles. To protect his legs from the dagger-like thorns, the Texas cowhand wore leather leggings called *chaparejos*, a Mexican-Spanish word that was shortened to 'chaps.'

OPPOSITE ABOVE LEFT: Oliver Loving, pioneer of the Goodnight-Loving Trail. CENTER: W J 'One-armed Jim' Wilson. RIGHT: Nelson Story, the cattleman. OPPOSITE BELOW: A few stores were to be found on the trail. Doan's Store was at a crossing of the Red River on the Western Trail.

The roundup was hard work and required all the cowboy's skills in driving out stubborn, half-wild Longhorns from brush and broken country, and in roping and branding them. Once corralled, the animals were deprived of food and water for several days, by which time they were much subdued and when released they were so preoccupied with the desire to drink that they did not run off into brush. Meanwhile, the mavericks were roped and branded. Unbranded calves kept close to their branded mothers and this signified ownership. Motherless calves or strays were called 'mavericks,' a name believed to have originated from the unbranded cattle owned by Colonel Sam Maverick, a Texas lawyer.

The story goes that in 1845 Maverick accepted a herd of cattle as payment of a debt and that he did little to look after them; the unmarked animals roamed far and wide and other ranchers took to adding this unbranded stock to their own herds. The term 'maverick' for an unbranded beast spread throughout the cattle country. It became a general rule that a cattleman was entitled to appropriate any maverick found on his range. There were, however, many disputes over such unbranded animals.

Crossing the Red River. A modern re-creation of a Texas longhorn trail drive from San Antonio, Texas to Dodge City, Kansas.

The introduction of barbed wire fences enabled ranchers to keep their cattle separated and ended the need for the old-time open range roundup.

A trail herd of 3,000 head was found to be the most manageable. Usually about ten cowboys, including the trail boss, or drover, were required to handle such a herd; the trail boss was hired by the cattle owner to drive his herd to market, the drover bought his cattle, driving them to market aided by hired cowhands. The cattle owner provided the horses, maybe six to a man, and the cowboy furnished his own saddle and bedding. The riders changed horses several times a day, for although cow ponies were hardy they would tire after three or four hours of constant activity. The job of looking after the remuda, the string of saddle horses held ready for use, was generally given to a youth learning to be a cowboy.

Cowhands were paid an average 30 dollars a month, the cook usually getting five dollars more. The trail boss, who bore full responsibil-

ity for the herd, received about 100 to 125 dollars a month, and probably a bonus at trail's end if he got the cattle to market with little loss. The cook drove the mess or chuckwagon, which carried the food, the bedrolls, and many other items necessary for the long journey. The chuckwagon was the focal point of a trail camp. Here the cowboys would eat and relax after the day's work, talk about the day's events, tell stories and sing traditional ditties. The cook was an important man and it did not do to upset him with a careless word or to complain about the chuck he prepared. If you were foolish enough to do so he could make life very unpleasant for you. There is the story of a canny cowboy who broke open a biscuit and said:
'It's burnt on the bottom and the top, it's raw in the middle and salty as hell—just the way I like 'em.'

The cattle were moved at the slow rate of ten to 15 miles a day, in a column about 50 feet wide and strung out nearly a mile long. 'The word "drive" is a misnomer as applied to the trail,' commented an article on the cattle trade in *Harper's New Monthly Magazine* of July 1884. 'It is exactly this which should *not* be done. Cattle . . . headed in the direction of their long journey, should be allowed to "drift" rather than be urged. Walking as they feed, they will accomplish their twelve or fifteen miles a day with but little exertion to themselves, and with very much less care and anxiety on the part of the herder.'

When properly handled the animals soon became accustomed to the trail routine and settled down, a dominant steer taking the lead and usually holding it throughout the trek. Some cattle owners had trained steers to regularly lead the others, such as Charles Goodnight's celebrated 'Old Blue,' who with a bell around

A photograph taken in the 1880s of a cowboy trail boss in Montana. He is shown fully equipped with lariat, rifle and revolver.

his neck headed drives for eight years; when he died Goodnight had his horns mounted in his ranch office. The more active animals would march near the front, the 'drags'—the weak or lazy cattle—in the rear.

Two top hands would ride 'point,' one on either side of the column's head to keep the herd on course, then came the 'swing' riders followed by the 'flank' riders who kept the cattle in line. 'Dragmen' were stationed along the rear sides of the herd to urge on the lagging animals and to prevent them from escaping. Riding drag was the worst job because of the clouds of thick dust kicked up by the herd. The task was usually given to new, inexperienced cowhands. Young Jim Herron, on joining the trail crew, considered himself 'the proudest boy in Texas. We headed north the next morning, me riding drag.' The trail boss or his assistant would ride 15 to 20 miles ahead of the column to scout for water, grass, and a campsite for the night.

'We always tried to reach water before sundown,' recalled Charles Goodnight to J Evetts Haley, in *Charles Goodnight: Cowman and Plainsman*. 'This gave us ample time to have the cattle filled and everything arranged for a pleasant night. The herd was put in a circle, the cattle being a comfortable distance apart. At first, when the cattle were fresh, I used a double guard; that is, half the men guarded the first part of the night, the other half the latter part. In storms or stampedes we were all on duty.'

A stampede, an ever present threat, usually occurred at night. The Longhorn, because of its wildness, was easily alarmed and quick to move. A sudden clap of thunder or other sharp noise, the smell of a wolf, the bark of a coyote, the sound of a rattlesnake, any of a host of things might bring some of the animals swiftly to their feet in fright, the fear would spread and suddenly the herd was running in blind panic. And no cattle can stampede like the Longhorn could; modern cross-breeds do not get scared, or have the ability to run like the wild Texas

cattle. Experienced trail drivers held the belief that if a herd could be kept from stampeding in the first week or so on the trail then the danger of one occurring was greatly diminished, the trail slogan being: the best way to handle a stampede is to try and prevent it happening.

'A good herd boss,' J Frank Dobie tells us in *The Longhorns*, 'would not bed his cattle on ground that sounded hollow, in a narrow valley, or on a rough point. He picked, if possible, the kind of level ground the cattle would pick for themselves for a bed. He kept the camp quiet and not too far away from the herd. He watered out the cattle thoroughly and saw that they got their fill of grass before lying down.'

The cowhands would sleep near the chuckwagon and its fire, taking turns to guard the cattle, for Longhorns had to be constantly watched throughout the night. Working two-hour shifts, two riders would circle the herd continuously, riding slowly in opposite directions, probably humming, whistling, or crooning in a low voice to reassure the nervous animals. Nearly all the old cowboy songs were slow, as slow as a night mount walks around sleeping cattle, and most of them were mournful. Night horses soon learned their duty and if a rider briefly fell asleep in the saddle the horse could be relied on to continue its leisurely pace. The cowboy often sang of his affinity with his horse. *I Ride an Old Paint* (a pinto) was a traditional song, a chorus of which went as follows:

Oh when I die, take my saddle off the wall,
Put it on my pony, lead him from his stall.
Tie my bones to his back, turn our faces to
   the West,
And we'll ride the prairies that we love the
   best.

Cowboys dreaded a stampede (from the Spanish *estampida*) chiefly because of the time and effort involved in reassembling the scattered herd. A stampede always resulted in the loss of some animals, and injuries inflicted on each other with their horns. And running for miles 'worked the tallow off them,' adversely affecting their market weight. Jim Herron recalled the dread of the stampede and the technique called 'milling' employed to bring the rushing beasts to a halt.

OPPOSITE TOP: *A photograph of a roundup and branding in Arizona in the early 1880s.* OPPOSITE BOTTOM: *Longhorns on a trail drive heading north from Texas in the 1870s, a detail taken from a painting by the American artist Tom Lea.*

'Stampedes were something frightful to see, and any man's knees will rattle when the big Longhorns start to run. There was nothing to do then but run with them, stay ahead of them if you could, and turn them into a tight mill when you got the chance, circle them until they was wound up as tight as an eight-day clock on Sunday. It took the best night horse to stay with them. Once, we rode alongside the leaders for five miles, then gathered cattle over that five-mile stretch all the next day.'

An' woe to the rider and woe to the steed,
That falls in front of the mad stampede.

It appears, however, that few cowboys were actually trampled to death in stampedes. Ab

Cowboy in a Stampede *by Frederic Remington.*

Blocker, veteran Texas trail boss, said that he 'never heard of a cowboy being run over in a stampede.' He maintained, as did others, that stampeding cattle, no matter how dark the night, would split and go around a man in front of them. It is said that more cowboys were killed by lightning than maddened steers. But it took courage to ride out a stampede on a black night over country full of gopher holes or prairie-dog burrows. Many a horse threw its rider after stepping into such a hole.

'What need to tell of the miseries of that dreadful night,' wrote drover and former Texas

Ranger R H Williams of a stampede in the 1860s. 'The wind and the rain buffeted and soaked us; the thunder rolled overhead almost incessantly, and the cattle became wilder and more terrified the more we tried to stay their headlong flight. Fortunately for me the country was open, rolling prairie for miles and miles; had it been brushy I should probably have lost the whole drove, at least temporarily. As it was when day at last broke, and we rounded up the cattle about twelve miles from camp, forty of them had disappeared.'

Rattlesnakes and scorpions were other, if minor, hazards of the trail drive and range life. Experienced cowboys always shook their boots out before pulling them on in case a scorpion might be lurking inside. A scorpion sting would not kill a man but it would cause him much pain. Rattlesnakes prefer dry regions and are mostly found in the southwest. All rattlesnakes—of which there are thirty species—are venomous but some are more dangerous to humans than others—the most deadly species being the western diamondback, the timber and the Mojave rattlesnakes. The bigger the snake the more lethal it is, because size determines its striking distance and the quality and quantity of its venom. When alarmed, or ready to strike, it vibrates its tail rattle, then lunges forward with its jaws open to the fullest extent, driving its long curved fangs deep into its victim, injecting venom through the hollow fangs. The venom can kill a man. The biggest rattler is the western diamondback, found from Texas to California, which grows to a length of some six feet.

The Texas cowboy learned from the Mexican *vaquero* that the poison of the Spanish dagger, a type of thorny plant, jabbed into the flesh near a rattlesnake bite, could neutralize the venom. Cowboys (who often wore snake skin bands around their hats) would either shoot rattlers or kill them with their quirts, or short whips. 'I generally killed them with my quirt,' a cowboy recalled in Thayer's *Marvels of the New West*, 1888, 'which is about 18 inches long, made of rawhide and leather plaited together, with a piece of iron in the handle. A snake cannot strike unless it first coils itself up, so you can hit it when it is gliding off, with even a short weapon, without fear of the consequences . . . One of my horses was once bitten right on the nose. His head swelled up tremendously and he could not eat for two or three days, but he ultimately recovered. When a man gets bitten, the cure chiefly relied on is copious doses of whiskey.'

Crossing a deep, wide river was always a difficult operation fraught with peril, only possible if the cattle had leaders to brave the way first. Once the Longhorns had taken the plunge they were good swimmers. Normally a cowboy

A Frederic Remington illustration of three cowboys and their horses struggling to pull a chuckwagon out of the mire.

would swim his horse ahead of the herd as an example. Having got the herd into the river and swimming for the opposite bank, there was always the danger of them stampeding in the water. A strange sound, a floating log or other flotsom, even a sudden eddy might spook the leading animals to turn about and suddenly the entire herd would be mixed up madly in the water. And the cowhands, risking life and limb, would have to untangle the terrified beasts and get them swimming together in the right direction. A number of cowboys were drowned in river crossings.

Dudley Snyder, of the famous Snyder brothers' cattle company, was noted for training two work oxen as lead swimmers. He would unyoke them at a stream and they would head the herd across. They never faltered in their duty, not even when faced with the intimidating expanse of the Mississippi (crossed on a drive during the Civil War), and the herd always followed them. Snyder kept secret his method of training his swimming oxen and, apparently, no other trail driver of later years managed to emulate the feat. The chuckwagon was either floated across with logs lashed to its wheels, or emptied and pulled across by ropes, the contents being rafted over.

The Red River was just one of ten rivers on the Chisholm Trail. But it had a special significance because it marked the boundary between Texas and the Indian Territory, the land reserved for Indian tribes removed from other states by the U S Government, that eventually formed part of Oklahoma when that state was created in 1907. In its low condition the sluggish river could be crossed at many points, the most popular place being Red River Station, where a shelving sandbar ran out from the northern bank and made it possible for cattle to walk across the river. On the Western Trail, Doan's Crossing was a favored spot; it was named after C F Doan who opened a store there to service the trail crews.

The ruthless destruction of the buffalo—which had once roamed the western prairies in their millions—by professional white hunters deprived the Indians of their chief means of sustenance. The well-ordered society of the Plains tribes was largely dependent on the all-providing buffalo, which gave the Indians meat, skins for tents and clothes, and horns and bones for weapons and tools. The Indians used every part of the beast, nothing was wasted. The white hunters, on the other hand, wiped out the great herds for the commercial value of their hides, leaving the meat to rot on the plains.

It was easy to shoot a buffalo from a safe distance. An experienced hunter could kill animals faster than a good skinner could remove the hides; hunters often killed 250 buffalo a day and many slaughtered up to 3000 a year. Having exterminated the southern herd, the professional hunters turned to the northern herd and, between 1876 and 1883, destroyed that also. The US military approved the mass slaughter as a means of depriving the troublesome Plains Indians of their staff of life, thus making it easy to subdue them. Cattlemen were also thankful that the swarming buffalo had been removed from the open ranges to make way for the growing population of beef livestock.

The tribes of the Indian Territory, wise to the laws of the white man, demanded a toll of ten cents a head on all cattle trailed through their land. The Texans grudgingly paid the tax or gave cattle in lieu of payment. The Indians, many of whom raised cattle themselves, also demanded the right to inspect the herds to see if any of their own animals had got mixed with the passing Longhorns. Some Texans refused to comply with the Indian demands and endeavored to strong-arm their way through. John Wesley Hardin, young trail boss and gunfighter, had a run-in with Osage braves on the Chisholm Trail in 1871. While he was absent from the camp the Osages had paid a visit; scaring the cook and some cowhands, they cut out a few cattle and departed, taking with them Hardin's prized silver bridle. So when a band of 20 warriors returned to take some more cattle, Hardin rode up to a big Indian riding a pony wearing the Texan's fancy bridle.

OPPOSITE TOP: A photograph of a cattle drive from New Mexico to Kansas taken in the 1880s by F M Steel.
OPPOSITE BOTTOM: A group of cowboys of the 1880s preparing to take their turns at standing night guard over the herd.

COPYRIGHT BY F. M. STEEL.

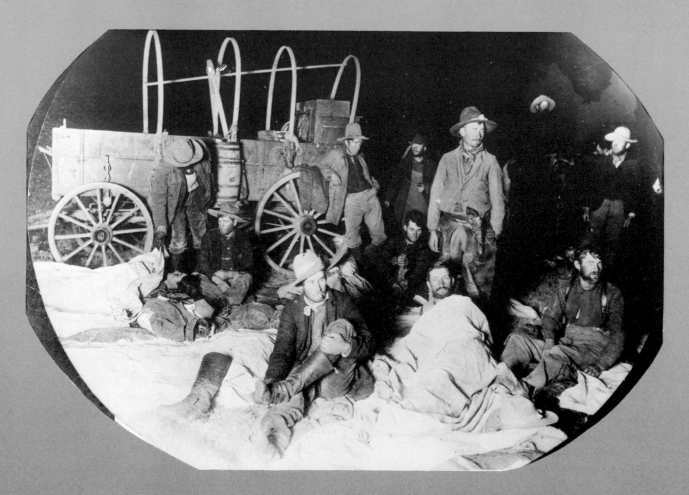

'I asked him how much he would take for it,' wrote Hardin in his autobiography, 'and offered him five dollars. He grunted an assent and gave me the bridle. When I got it, I told him that [it] was my bridle and someone had stolen it from camp that morning. He frowned and grunted and started to get the bridle back . . . I jabbed him with my pistol and when this would not stop him, I struck him over the head with it. He fell back and yelled to his companions. This put the devil in them. They came up in a body and demanded cattle again. I told them "no" as I had done before. An Indian rode to the herd and cut out a big beef steer. I told him to get out of the herd and pulled my pistol to emphasize my remarks. He was armed and drew his, saying that if I did not let him cut the beef out, he would kill the animal. I told him that if he killed the animal, I would kill him. Well, he killed the beef and I killed him. The other Indians promptly vanished. If they had not, there would have been more dead Indians.'

The ferocious Comanches of Texas were not so easily dealt with as were the subdued tribes of the Indian Territory. For nearly 200 years they had waged war against the Spaniards in Mexico, and they became bitter enemies of the Texans who had taken their best hunting grounds and fought them relentlessly for almost forty years. The Comanches plagued the Goodnight-Loving Trail that ran west through Texas, then north into New Mexico and Colorado. The Indian raiders sometimes managed to run off whole herds. In July, 1867 a war party of Comanches attacked Oliver Loving, trail-driving partner of Charles Goodnight, while he was riding far ahead of the herd.

With the whooping warriors chasing them, Loving and his cowboy companion, one-armed Bill Wilson, raced for the Pecos River, where they took up a defensive position in the tall canebreaks. They managed to hold off the Indians but Loving was hit by a bullet in the wrist and the side. When darkness fell, Loving, convinced he was dying, implored Wilson to save himself. Wilson reluctantly agreed, on the understanding that he would find help and return for his injured boss. Stripping to his underwear, the one-armed cowboy floated downriver, out of reach of the besieging Comanches. The bootless Wilson walked for several days until he met up with Goodnight and the herd. When a rescue party reached the place where Loving had been hiding, he could not be found.

Two weeks later Goodnight learned that his wounded partner had dragged himself five miles away, where he was picked up by Mexicans and taken to Fort Sumner, New Mexico. When Goodnight arrived at the fort he found Loving on the way to recovery, but soon after an infection of the wound proved fatal. Goodnight thought highly of his dead partner and friend and the next year gave his widow 40,000 dollars, half of the profit he had cleared on the cattle deals. The fierce Comanches were not subdued until 1874 when the military mounted a determined campaign against them.

Nelson Story drove his herd through country thick with hostile Sioux on a marathon drive of 1500 miles that took six months to complete. After making some money in the gold fields of Montana, Story decided to invest his capital in cattle. Having purchased 1000 Longhorns at Fort Worth, Texas, he trailed them with hired hands to Missouri, where he was stopped by the human barrier of armed farmers and grangers.

BELOW LEFT: Taking the Robe, *a painting by Frederic Remington.* BELOW RIGHT: Fight for the Waterhole, *also by Frederic Remington.*

Instead of trying to force or buy his way through to Sedalia, Story determined to drive his herd all the way to Montana where he knew he could sell the beeves to the gold miners at a high profit.

He headed the cattle west, then swung north and veered east to reach Fort Leavenworth, where he purchased wagons and oxen to pull them, and hired bull whackers to handle the teams. He loaded the wagons with stores and provisions and, together with the cattle, rolled west along the Oregon Trail to Fort Laramie, Wyoming, where he learned that the Sioux were on the warpath and that it would be highly dangerous to continue through the Powder River country. Nevertheless, Story was fixed on reaching Montana. He armed his twenty-seven men with the latest Remington breech-loaded, rapid-fire rifles and headed north.

Near Fort Reno, Story's caravan was pounced upon by a party of Sioux. They wounded two cowboys with arrows and ran off part of the herd. Story and his men followed the Indians, and when the redskins made camp, the cowboys hit them hard and fast with the new rifles and got back all the cattle. Story pressed on to Fort Phil Kearny, in what is now northern Wyoming. Here, the post commander, Colonel Carrington, told Story that to proceed through Sioux country would mean certain death for him and his crew. He ordered Story to halt near the fort and wait for permission to continue. The cowboys

A scene of a roundup from a sketch by Fenzeny and Tavernier in Harper's Weekly *of 2 May 1874.*

had to corral the cattle several miles from the fort because the soldiers required all the grass near the fort for their own animals.

Story was in a most unfavorable situation. If the Indians attacked his caravan in force the soldiers were too far away to give any assistance. And if he delayed his journey too long the snows would completely close the trail. That would entail wintering at the fort and selling his cattle cheaply to the soldiers. He decided to take his chances on the trail and his men agreed with him. At night, the wagons and cattle managed to pass the fort without being detected. Attacked several times by small bands of Sioux, the party fought them off, thanks to their rapid-firing Remingtons, and suffered only one death, a hunter riding ahead of the caravan, who was captured by the Indians, scalped and 'pincushioned' with arrows.

Six weeks after pushing on from Fort Phil Kearny, the caravan arrived at its destination, Virginia City, on 9 December 1866, where eager buyers snapped up the provisions and the cattle, paying 100 dollars a head for the Longhorns that Nelson Story had purchased for 10 dollars a head.

Dodge City, Kansas in the 1880s. The sign in the foreground informs visiting cowboys that 'The Carrying of Fire Arms' is 'Strictly Prohibited.'

3
THE
CATTLE
TOWNS

We all hit town and we hit her on the fly,
We bedded down the cattle on a hill close by.
We rounded 'em up and put 'em on the cars,
And that was the last of the old Two Bars.
                    The Old Chisholm Trail, cowboy song

On completion of the trail drive, the cattle sales were concluded, and the animals were penned and loaded into the railroad cars. The cowhands collected their hard earned pay and cut loose in the town. Having endured the rigors, the monotony and deprivations of the long ride, the young cowboy, dirty and dry, with about 100 dollars burning a hole in his pocket, was primed to blow the lot on a wild spree of drinking, dancing, whoring and gambling. And the opportunists and entrepreneurs attracted to the cowtowns provided ample facilities to cater to the cowboy's simple needs.

The Kansas cattle towns of Abilene, Ellsworth, Newton and Wichita all enjoyed a brief period of rip-roaring celebrity. Dodge City, 'Queen of the Cowtowns,' spawned history and legend for ten hectic years, 1875-85. And the law officers who managed to keep the peace in these anarchic boom towns have, over the years, attained the status of folk heroes. These violent, licentious railhead towns gave real meaning to the appellation 'Wild West.' Dressed in their flamboyant finery, toting their revolvers, the cowboys invaded the town intent on showing off and having a good time. After a visit to a barbershop, then perhaps to a photographer's studio to have souvenir pictures taken with their trail buddies, the Texans flung themselves into the fleshpots with amazing exultation.

'The cowboy enters the dance with a peculiar zest,' wrote Joseph McCoy, pioneer promoter of Abilene, 'not stopping to divest himself of his sombrero, spurs, or pistols, but just as he dismounts from his cow-pony so he goes into the dance . . . his huge spurs jingling at every step or motion; his revolvers flapping up and down . . . his eyes lit up with excitement and liquor, he plunges in and "hoes it down" at a terrible rate, in the most approved yet awkward country style, often swinging his "partner" clean off the floor.'

Abilene was the first of the famous Kansas cattle towns and it set the pattern for the others

One of the most popular places to relax was the saloon. These cowboys of the 1890s are drinking in a Texas bar.

Games of chance were also popular. These trail hands are playing faro in Morenci, Arizona Territory in 1895.

that followed. It served as a busy, bellowing shipping point from where, during the period 1867 to 1872, some 1½ million Longhorns were sent by railroad to the Kansas City and Chicago meat dressing plants. First settled in 1856, Abilene remained a quiet hamlet of a dozen cabins until 1867 when Illinois cattle dealer Joseph McCoy decided that the place would make the ideal site for a cattle terminus (the railroad had reached Abilene that year). McCoy had heard about the difficulties encountered by the Texas drovers trailing to the railhead at Sedalia, Missouri; the cowboys had been plagued by cattle thieves and attacked by angry farmers, the latter intent on turning back the herds for fear that the Longhorns would bring the dreaded Texas or Mexican cattle fever.

McCoy observed that another trail and another railhead were required, an isolated spot away from the sensitive populated regions. 'Abilene was selected,' he explains in his *Historic Sketches of the Cattle Trade of the West and Southwest, 1874*, 'because the country was entirely unsettled, well watered, had excellent

grass, and nearly the entire area of country was adapted to holding cattle. And it was the farthest point east at which a good depot for cattle business could have been made.'

He bought 250 acres on the edge of the settlement, built the three-story Drover's Cottage hotel, erected cattle pens, loading chutes, barns and livery stables. When all was ready, McCoy sent word to the cattlemen and buyers that Abilene was the place to meet and do business in safety. He publicized the route pioneered by the old halfbreed trader Jesse Chisholm, and the Chisholm Trail became the main cattle route from Texas to Kansas. That first year Abilene received 35,000 cattle, 75,000 in 1868, 350,000 in 1869, 300,000 in 1870, and 700,000 in 1871.

The town quickly became notorious for its lawlessness and vice. 'I have seen many fast towns,' commented John Wesley Hardin, cowboy and gunfighter, 'but I think Abilene beats

LEFT, TOP TO BOTTOM: Luke Short, the gambler and dangerous gunman; 'Rowdy Joe' Lowe, the saloon keeper and gunfighter; Bat Masterson, the marshal of Dodge City; James Butler 'Wild Bill' Hickok when he was marshal of Abilene, Kansas; Tom Smith, one-time marshal of Abilene. OPPOSITE ABOVE: The famous Long Branch Saloon in Dodge City. OPPOSITE BELOW: Wichita in the 1870s.

them all. The town was filled with sporting men and women, gamblers, cowboys, desperadoes and the like. It was well-supplied with bar rooms, hotels, barber shops and gambling houses, and everything was open.' Abilene was divided by the railroad into two sections: the north side of the track housed the respectable element, the churches, banks, newspaper office and several large stores. The south side accommodated the hotels, saloons and gambling dens. 'When you are on the north side,' stated the Topeka *Kansas State Record*, describing Abilene in 1871, 'you are in Kansas, and hear sober and profitable conversation on the subject of the weather, the price of land and the crops; when you cross to the south side you are in "Texas," and talk about cattle . . . five at least out of every ten [men you meet] are Texans.'

The lads from the Lone Star State were a wild and whooping lot indeed, who delighted in charging up and down the boardwalks on their ponies, barging into saloon and dance hall, shooting out the lights, and using their guns on anybody daring or foolish enough to oppose their belligerent antics. Clearly, something had to be done to contain and control these Texas terrors who, if not restrained, might eventually dominate the entire township. A marshal was needed, but he would have to be a very brave and able man. Theodore C Henry, Abilene's first mayor, made the right choice in 'Bear River' Tom Smith.

Smith was unusual in that he preferred to use his fists instead of guns to subdue a troublemaker. And he could use his fists with remarkable ability. Cowboys and frontiersmen did not resort to fisticuffs to settle an argument—a gun or knife concluded the difference once and for all. The new marshal's flying fists came as a jolting and sobering surprise to the swaggering Texans. Hardly anything is known about Smith before his years out West. It is said that he hailed from New York where he was a prize

fighter and later a member of the police force. This would certainly account for his fistic ability. In 1868 he established a reputation as a peace officer at Bear River, Wyoming, one of the 'hell-on-wheels' towns that followed the construction gangs of the Union Pacific Railroad. Henceforth he was known as 'Bear River' Tom Smith.

He became Abilene's chief of police on 4 June 1870. A broad-shouldered middleweight, nearly six feet tall, he was never known to back away from trouble. He immediately began to enforce the town's ordinance that forbade the carrying of firearms—a sensitive point with gun-proud Texans. Smith knocked down a lot of cowboys who, on being asked calmly and politely to give up their guns, refused to comply. Tom socked them hard and took their weapons.

On one occasion, on hearing shots from a saloon, he went to investigate. He walked through the only door and there at the far end of the narrow room was a drunken Texan brandishing his pistol. As Tom walked toward the man he noticed that other cowboys had crowded in front of the door, cutting off his exit. He did not hesitate in his action. Confronting the drunk, he drew his Colt and smashed it over the man's head, knocking him senseless. Stunned for a moment at the lawman's audacity, the other Texans pulled their shooting irons. Tom picked up the unconscious man, slung him over his shoulder and walked out; the cowboys would not shoot for fear of hitting their comrade.

Tom Smith managed to tame the Texans, who came to admire and respect the resolute peace officer who did not kill cowboys. The Abilene *Chronicle* of 8 September 1870 reported that 'The respectable citizens of Abilene may well feel proud of the order and quietness now prevailing in the town . . . Chief of Police T J Smith and his assistants . . . deserve the thanks of the people for the faithful and prompt manner in which they have discharged their official duties.' Sad to relate, the valiant Smith was killed while making an arrest in November 1870, murdered not by wild Texans but by two settlers outside the town's limits. The men were later captured and sentenced to long terms of imprisonment. 'Although our people will never again permit the lawlessness which existed prior to his [Smith's] coming to town,' the *Chronicle* commented, 'yet it will be a long time before his equal will be found in all the essentials required to make a model police officer.'

The man chosen to replace Smith was James Butler 'Wild Bill' Hickok, a lawman of the gunfighter type, born in 1837 in Illinois. An impressive figure, over six feet tall, with shoulder-length hair, he wore fashionable city clothes and always carried two Colt revolvers stuck into a belt or silk sash. He was a marksman, cool and courageous in a dangerous situation, having previously killed a number of men in shoot-outs. His career out West had included jobs as a stagecoach and freight driver; he served the Union Army in the Civil War as a scout, wagonmaster, and spy. He is said to have won his famous sobriquet 'Wild Bill' by stopping a mob, single handed, from lynching a man. He gained fame when an account of his exploits, based on an interview with Colonel George Ward Nichols, was published in *Harper's New Monthly Magazine* of February, 1867.

Hickok was sworn in as marshal of Abilene on 15 April 1871 at a salary of 150 dollars a month. Wild Bill was a man who trod carefully, his eyes alert for any hostile move, and he never took chances. 'He *slid* into a room,' recalled an old-timer, 'keeping his back to the wall, watching the whole crowd like a hawk. He looked like a man who lived in expectation of getting killed.'

Texas cowboy Brown Paschal recalled his first impression of Hickok. 'He came out of Ben Thompson's Bull's Head saloon. He wore a low-crowned, wide black hat and a frock coat. His hair was yellow and it hung down to his shoulders . . . He was standing there with his back to the wall, his thumbs hooked in his red sash. He stood there and rolled his head from side to side looking at everything and everybody . . . just like a mad old bull. I decided then and there that I didn't want any part of him.'

Wild Bill's reputation helped keep the peace in Abilene. While marshal there he was involved in only one recorded shooting incident. On 5 October 1871 Hickok was having a drink with his friend Mike Williams in the Novelty Bar when he heard a shot in the street. Telling

Williams to stay put, Hickok went to investigate, and outside the Alamo saloon confronted a crowd of armed cowboys headed by Phil Coe, a tall Texan gambler and co-owner of the Bull's Head. Coe told the marshal that he had fired at a dog. There was bad blood between Hickok and Coe; Hickok had been told that Coe intended to kill him. Wild Bill ordered the Texans to give up their guns. Coe pointed his pistol at Hickok.

'Quick as thought,' reported the *Chronicle*, 'the Marshal drew two revolvers and both men

fired almost simultaneously.' At that precise moment someone rushed between Hickok and Coe and stopped the marshal's bullets. Coe fired twice, one passing between Wild Bill's legs, the other piercing his coat tail. Hickok fired both guns again, hitting Coe in the stomach and dropping him. Bill covered the other Texans, saying: 'If any of you want the balance of these pills, come and get them!' There were no takers, and Bill added: 'Now all you mount your ponies and ride for camp, and do it damn quick!' Then Hickok found to his horror that

Faro Players by W L Dodge. This scene in a smoky saloon shows the dealer wearing his top hat and having his Derringer revolver on the table. Many of the cowboys are wearing their holstered guns.

the man who had run between him and Coe at the moment of shooting was Mike Williams, who had come to aid the marshal. Coe died after several days of agony.

With the end of the cattle season, the Abilene city council decided to dispense with the ex-

After driving their herd to Montana, these Texans of the XIT outfit relaxed and had their picture taken in Miles City.

pensive services of Hickok and in December, 1871 appointed J A Gauthie as marshal at 50 dollars a month. Now that their town was firmly established, the good citizens of Abilene decided they could do without the troublesome Texas cattle trade, no matter how lucrative it might be, and in February, 1872 notice was served on the Texas cattlemen 'to seek some other point for shipment, as the inhabitants of Dickinson [County] will no longer submit to the evils of the trade.'

Ellsworth, another railhead on the Kansas Pacific Railway, served as a major cattle town from 1871 to 1873 and, like all places of its kind, it gained a fierce reputation. Laid out in the spring of 1867, the town boasted the biggest stockyards in Kansas, and the only solid sidewalk—made of limestone rock—west of Kansas City in the plains country; the sidewalk was 12 feet wide and ran the length of the Grand Central Hotel, favored house of the top cattlemen. To the east of the town stood the community of Nauchville, the red light district.

Among the gamblers and other social parasites who came to Ellsworth to profit from the

officers were not always chosen for their integrity, but often for their gunfighting ability), and was shot dead in San Antonio in 1884 over a gambling feud.

Gambling was the cowboy's—and the frontiersman's—chief means of recreation. It provided company, excitement and the chance to win a big stake. Card games were the most popular and these included seven-up, blackjack, monte, poker, and faro, the latter known out West as 'bucking the tiger'; William 'Bucky' O'Neill, noted sheriff of Yavapai County, Arizona in the 1880s, won his nickname because of his addiction to faro. Wild Bill Hickok, Bat Masterson, and Wyatt Earp were inveterate gamblers. Hickok was killed—shot in the back—while playing poker, and the five cards that he held at the time included the ace of spades, ace of clubs, eight of clubs, eight of spades, and these 'aces and eights' became known to poker players as the 'Dead Man's Hand.'

Every cattle town and frontier settlement had its gambling houses. Gambling was, to quote Bat Masterson, 'not only the principal and best-paying industry of the town, but was also reckoned among its most respectable.' Professional gamblers who drifted from town to town included Ben Thompson, John Henry 'Doc' Holliday, and Luke Short, all of them skilled in the use of firearms. Luke Short was born in Mississippi and grew up in Texas. As a working cowhand he trailed a herd up to Kansas and became fascinated by the gambling action at Abilene. Preferring poker to poking cows he became a professional gaming man. A small, dapper figure he was, like Doc Holliday, deadly with a gun. Luke carried his short-barreled .45 Colt in a special leather-lined pocket designed so that it did not spoil the hang of his elegant frock coat.

Unlike Holliday, who had a quick temper, cool hand Luke had a long fuse. When a braggart named Brown leaned over the faro table and moved Luke's chips, saying, 'Play it that way, Shorty,' the little gambler let it pass. When Brown repeated his interference Luke warned him to stay away. The troublemaker stepped back, cursing, and went for his gun. But Luke was faster and shot him. Charlie Storms, another professional gambler, once

free-spending Texans was the celebrated Ben Thompson, a gunfighter credited with 32 killings. British-born Thompson was co-owner with Phil Coe of the Bull's Head saloon in Abilene; when Coe was killed by Hickok, Ben was out of town. At Ellsworth, Ben was joined by his hare-brained brother Billy, who caused a lot of trouble in the town. When Billy's drunken gunplay brought Sheriff Chauncey Whitney to the scene, Billy mortally wounded him with a shotgun blast. Ben held off the enraged onlookers while Billy rode out of town. He was brought to trial in 1877 and acquitted. Ben was later elected marshal of Austin, Texas (peace

To the cowboys, the bartender in the saloon of a western town was one of the more important citizens. This rough and ready barkeeper was painted by Olaf C Seltzer.

threw chips into Luke's face over a losing turn of the cards. Storms was the worse for drink and again Luke let the incident pass. Some years later, however, when Storms ran into Short in Tombstone, Arizona, he attempted to shoot him at close range but, according to eyewitness Bat Masterson, 'he was too slow. He got his pistol out, but Luke stuck the muzzle of his own pistol against Storms' heart and pulled the trigger . . . and as he was falling, Luke shot him again. Storms was dead when he hit the ground.'

Newton followed the pattern of the other Kansas cattle towns. Founded in March, 1871 it became a terminus of the Chisholm Trail when the Atchison, Topeka and Santa Fe Railroad reached the town in July that year. By the end of 1871 some 30,000 head of cattle had been shipped out of the place. Newton flourished under the usual clouds of Texan gunsmoke. Cal Johnston, a long-time resident of the town, recalled that the shooting 'was so continuous that it reminded me of a Fourth of July celebration from daylight to midnight. There was shooting when I got up and when I went to bed.' Newton's brothel district was known as 'Hide Park.'

When policeman Mike McCluskie shot a Texan during a quarrel, the killing triggered the shoot-out known as 'Newton's General Massacre.' It took place in the early hours of Sunday, 20 August 1871. A group of cowboy friends of the dead Texan confronted McCluskie in a dance hall. And according to a report in *The Kansas Daily Commonwealth*, one of them said to McCluskie: 'You are a cowardly son of a bitch! I will blow the top of your head off!' And promptly shot the policeman in the neck, and when he fell, shot him again in the back. Then it seemed that everybody in the crowded place started shooting. When the gunfire ended, nine bodies littered the blood-spattered dance hall. McCluskie and four others died, the rest were injured.

The *Commonwealth* called it the 'most terrible tragedy that has ever occurred in Kansas during civil times. It is a burning shame and disgrace to Kansas, and measures should be at once adopted to prevent a repetition.' The paper went on to say that as the town's authorities could not keep the peace, the army should be called in and martial law declared. The violence went on. Lawmen came and went with little result. The town continued to disgrace Kansas until 1873, when the railroad reached

ABOVE: *The painting,* Drifters, *by Charles M Russell, captures the loneliness of the cowboy life.*

BELOW: *A bronco-busting scene painted by Frederic Remington, entitled* Turn Him Loose, Bill.

ABOVE: *Cattle arriving at Dodge City, Kansas.* LEFT: *An illustration by Frederic Remington showing a gunfight in a saloon.* BELOW LEFT: *Dance hall girls were always ready to help the trail hands enjoy themselves. Here are Texas cowboys in Dodge City.* BELOW RIGHT: *Some cowboys overdid things at the end of a trail drive. This is an example of cowboy fun in a Kansas cowtown.*

Wichita, which supplanted 'Shootin' Newton' as a cattle and trouble center.

Wichita held the dubious distinction of being the roughest, toughest cowtown in Kansas for two years, 1873 and 1874. Like other cattle towns it had its good and bad sections. The bad or cowboy section was called Delano, or West Wichita, situated on the opposite bank of the Arkansas from Wichita proper. City authority did not extend beyond the river and therefore Delano was lawless. 'Rowdy Joe' Lowe, who with his wife 'Rowdy Kate,' ran a dance hall-saloon-brothel in Delano, was stalwart enough to act as his own policeman. If a customer started trouble, Rowdy Joe would promptly knock the nonsense out of him. He had owned similar establishments in Ellsworth and Newton.

'His dance hall [in Delano] is patronized mainly by cattle herders, though all classes visit it; the respectable mostly from curiosity,' reported the *Commonwealth*. 'The Texan, with mammoth spurs on his boots . . . and broad-brimmed sombrero on his head, is seen dancing by the side of a well-dressed, gentlemanly-appearing stranger from some eastern city; both having painted and jeweled courtesans for partners. In the corner of the hall are seen gamblers playing at their favorite game of poker.' A rival establishment was run by E T 'Red' Beard, who sported shoulder-length red hair.

On 3 June 1873 an argument erupted in Red Beard's place between a soldier of the Sixth Cavalry and a woman of the house over a matter of five dollars. The soldier drew his gun and shot the lady through the thigh. Red Beard reacted like the gentleman he was. 'As soon as the shot was fired,' related the *Commonwealth*, 'Red instantly drew his self-cocking revolver and commenced an indiscriminate fusilade, shooting two soldiers . . . The soldiers who were shot [and wounded] were not engaged in the quarrel, and are spoken of by their comrades as being very quiet and gentlemanly. The soldier who commenced the affray escaped unhurt and deserted [his regiment] last night.' A few days later the comrades of the wounded soldiers marched in force on Red Beard's dance hall and set fire to it.

The rivalry between Red and Rowdy Joe ex-ploded into a shoot-out in October 1873; Rowdy was wounded in the neck and Red in the arm and hip. Beard died of his wounds. Rowdy Joe was later shot dead.

By 1874 Wichita was the leading cattle shipping center, with 200,000 cattle and 2,000 cowboys flooding into the area at the height of the season. The Wichita *Eagle* of 28 May 1874 commented that though 'the cattle season has not yet fully set in . . . there is a rush of gamblers and harlots who are lying in wait for the [cowboy] game which will soon begin to come up from the south.' Wyatt Earp was appointed policeman on the Wichita force in April 1875 but never became marshal. In May 1876 Earp joined the police force of Dodge City, which replaced Wichita as the premier cattle town in 1875 and reigned as 'Queen of the Cowtowns' for ten flamboyant years.

Founded in 1872 some five miles west of Fort Dodge, the army post built in 1864, Dodge City was originally a buffalo hunters' town. With millions of buffalo within hunting range, some 1½ million hides were shipped east from Dodge on the Atchison, Topeka and Santa Fe Railroad. In its early years as the 'Cowboy Capital,' Dodge City was noted for its licentiousness and violence. There is the apocryphal story of the young cowboy who, after a rough night at Newton, got on the train. 'Where do you want to go?' asked the conductor.

'To Hell, I guess,' replied the surly cowboy.

'Well, give me two dollars 50 and get off at Dodge.'

When law and order was established in this turbulent town, its peace officers were celebrated for their excellence, in particular the three redoubtable Masterson brothers, Edward, James, and Bartholomew, the latter better known as 'Bat.' It soon proved to be a town the Texans could not take over and run to suit themselves. 'Don't ever get the impression that you can ride your horses into a saloon, or shoot out the lights in Dodge,' the veteran trail driver advised the young cowhands in Andy Adams' *The Log of a Cowboy*, 1903. 'It may go somewhere else, but it don't go there. So I want to warn you to behave yourselves. You can wear your six-shooters into town, but you'd better leave them at the first place you stop . . . And when you

leave town ... don't ride out shooting ... for your six-shooters are no match for Winchesters and buckshot; and Dodge's [peace] officers are as game a set of men as ever faced danger.'

Edward J. Masterson, eldest of the brothers, was appointed assistant marshal in June, 1877. The Dodge City *Times* remarked that 'He is not very large, but there are not many men who would be anxious to tackle him a second time. He makes a good officer.' In attempting to stop a man named Bob Shaw from killing 'Texas Dick' Moore, Masterson was shot and wounded by Shaw. As Ed fell he returned the fire and hit Shaw in the arm and leg, putting him out of action. Both men recovered and Shaw left Dodge, never to return. Ed Masterson did his duty with distinction and in December, 1877 was promoted to marshal.

On 9 April 1878 Ed disarmed a drunken cowboy named Jack Wagner and handed the sixgun to Wagner's trail boss, Alfred Walker, for safe keeping. A little later, in company with deputy marshal Hayward, Masterson met Wagner again on the sidewalk and saw that he was wearing a gun. Ed went to take possession of the weapon. As Hayward stepped in to assist his chief in the struggle, other Texans stopped him at gunpoint. Wagner fired his revolver into Masterson's stomach, being so close that the discharge flash set the marshal's clothes on fire.

Despite his fatal wound, Ed managed to draw his own gun and shoot Wagner, and also Walker, who had entered the fight. Masterson stumbled into Hoover's saloon and said to the bartender, 'George, I'm shot,' then sank to the floor, his clothes still burning. Ed died 30 minutes later. Meanwhile, Wagner had staggered into another saloon and collapsed; he died the next day. Walker, wounded in the lung and right arm, recovered and returned to Texas.

Gunfight *by Charles M Russell.* INSET: *The shiny brass star of a United States Deputy Marshal in Oklahoma.*

'The death of Marshal Masterson caused great feeling in Dodge City,' reported the Dodge City *Times*. 'The business houses were draped in mourning and business on Wednesday generally suspended. Elsewhere we give expression of sympathy and ceremonies following this terrible tragedy.'

In June 1878 Jim Masterson, youngest of the brothers, joined the Dodge City police department, of which Wyatt Earp was assistant marshal. Jim served as marshal from 1879 to 1881. He and Earp were on duty the night Dora Hand was shot. James Kenedy, cowboy son of a wealthy Texas cattleman, had a grudge against James 'Dog' Kelley, the mayor of Dodge, and decided to kill him. In the early morning hours he rode up to Kelley's two-room cabin and fired his revolver into it, hoping to hit his sleeping victim. He did. His victim, however, was not Kelley but the unfortunate Dora Hand, also known as Fannie Keenan, an actress popular in Dodge. Unknown to Kenedy, Kelley had fallen ill and had been taken away for treatment, leaving the use of his cabin to Dora and another actress. Poor Dora had been sleeping in the mayor's bed and was killed instantly by the shots. Kenedy was seen galloping out of town and a posse was soon after him.

The posse consisted of Bat Masterson, then serving as sheriff of Ford County; his deputy Bill Duffy; Charles Bassett, marshal of Dodge;

A cowboy band in Dodge City, Kansas in 1886.

Wyatt Earp and Bill Tilghman, 'as intrepid a posse as ever pulled a trigger,' commented the Dodge City *Times*. After a long ride they caught up with Kenedy, who was armed with a brace of pistols, a carbine, and a Bowie knife, and brought him back to Dodge in a wounded condition. At his examination before Judge Cook, Kenedy was acquitted for lack of evidence; that is to say, nobody actually saw him fire the shots. Dora Hand was given a fine funeral and buried in the new Prairie Grove Cemetery, north of the town.

'Most places are satisfied with one abode for the dead. In the grave there is no distinction,' the Dodge City *Times* had intoned in September 1877, 'and yet Dodge boasts two burying spots, one for the tainted, whose very souls were steeped by immorality, and who have generally died with their boots on. "Boot Hill' is the somewhat singular title applied to [this] burial place. The other is not designated by any particular title, but is supposed to contain the bodies of those who died with a clean sheet on their bed.'

Bat Masterson was a favorite son of Dodge City. He was there in its formative years as a buffalo hunter. After serving as a police officer in Dodge he was elected in November, 1877 as sheriff of Ford County, of which Dodge City was the county seat, and he brought in a number of badmen to stand trial. Bat was justly celebrated in his own time, unlike his friend and colleague Wyatt Earp, who gained his legendary fame after he died, chiefly through his highly imaginative 'biography' written (and some say mostly invented) by journalist Stuart N Lake and published in 1931. The Leavenworth, Kansas, *Times* of 28 January 1879 described Bat as 'one of the most noted men of the southwest, as cool, brave and daring as anyone who ever drew a pistol.' Billy Dixon, famous frontiersman, likened Bat to 'a chunk of steel' and 'anything that struck him in those days always drew fire.'

Bat's exploits are too numerous to relate here but one in particular should be included because it demonstrates the shifting fortunes of lawmen-gunfighters of the period. In April 1881 Jim Masterson, now ex-marshal, was a partner of A J Peacock in a dance hall and saloon business in Dodge. Jim had an argument with Peacock which resulted in guns being drawn and shots fired, Peacock being backed by his bartender Al Updegraff, but no one was hurt. At that time Bat, no longer a peace officer, was at Tombstone, Arizona, prospecting for gold. Jim telegraphed his brother asking him to return to Dodge and help him in his difficulties.

Bat came on the first train and immediately confronted Peacock and Updegraff in the street. At a distance of 20 feet he called to them: 'I have come over a thousand miles to settle this. I know you are heeled [armed]. Now fight.' All three started firing, then they took cover and continued shooting for about five minutes until their guns were empty. Updegraff was the only one hurt, shot through the lungs (fortunately he recovered). Bat was arrested by police officers and fined 10 dollars and costs for disturbing the peace.

'Great indignation was manifested and is still felt by the citizens against the Masterson party,' thundered the *Ford County Globe*, 'as the shooting was caused by a private quarrel, and the parties who were anxious to fight should have had at least a thought for the danger they were causing disinterested parties on the street and in business houses . . . the citizens are thoroughly aroused and will not stand any more foolishness. They will not wait for the law to take its course if such an outrage should again occur.'

Nevertheless, the good citizens of Dodge forgave their favorite, if wayward, son and in the Fourth of July celebration of 1885, the genial Bat was elected the 'Most Popular Man in Dodge' and was presented with a gold-headed cane that he carried proudly for many years. With Dodge changing its character from wild young cowtown to mature respectability, Bat said goodbye to the place and drifted to other parts of the West. In 1902 he settled in New York City and became a successful sports writer on the *Morning Telegraph*. He died at his desk from a heart attack in 1921.

During the cattle boom of the late 1870s and early 1880s more than 250,000 head a year were shipped from Dodge. Not all the herds trailed into Dodge were sent east on the railroad, many were 'through cattle' that were driven on up to the northern ranges of Montana, Wyoming, and the Dakotas. Dodge City's rollicking reign as Queen of the Cowtowns ended in 1885 when the long-threatened quarantine line, under mounting pressure from the farmers, was extended all the way to the western border of the state, and Texas cattle were forbidden to enter Kansas.

'Wild Bill' Hickok was shot dead by Jack McCall while playing poker in a saloon in Deadwood City, Dakota Territory. He was holding what came to be known as the 'Dead Man's Hand' —two pair, aces and eights.

The Pierce-Arrow

INDEX

ACKNOWLEDGMENTS

The author and publisher would like to thank the following people who have helped in the preparation of this book: Anistatia Vassilopoulos, who designed it; Thomas G Aylesworth, who edited it; Karin Knight, who prepared the index.

PICTURE CREDITS

All pictures were supplied by Peter Newark's **Western Americana.** The author would like to thank the following:
Amoco Oil Co: 13 (main).
California Historical Society: 26–27.
Colt Industries Firearms Div: 18, 19 (top).
The Dobie Collection, University of Texas, Austin: 33 (center above).
Elfriede Hueber: 7.
Kansas State Historical Society: 41, 44–45, 48, 49, 60.
Kennedy Galleries, Inc, New York City: 31 (inset), 55 (below).
Library of Congress: 35.
Montana Historical Society: 52–53.
National Park Service, US Dept of the Interior: 18 (top), 19 (below right).
Oliver Yates Collection: 13, 22, 33 (above right), 42 (right).
Title Insurance and Trust Co, Los Angeles: 19 (below left).
University of Texas, El Paso: 11 (center).
Woolaroc Museum, Bartlesville, Okla: 1, 16 (top), 19 (top).
Wyoming State Archives and Historical Dept: 2–3.